Gifts from the Mountain

Gifts from the Mountain
Simple Truths for Life's Complexities

Eileen McDargh

Illustrations by Roderick MacIver

BERRETT-KOEHLER PUBLISHERS, INC.
San Francisco
a BK Life book

Berrett-Koehler Publishers, Inc.
235 Montgomery Street, Suite 650
San Francisco, CA 94104-2916
Tel: (415) 288-0260   Fax: (415) 362-2512   www.bkconnection.com

Ordering Information
Quantity sales. Special discounts are available on quantity purchases by corporations, associations, and others. For details, contact the "Special Sales Department" at the Berrett-Koehler address above.

Individual sales. Berrett-Koehler publications are available through most bookstores. They can also be ordered directly from Berrett-Koehler: Tel: (800) 929-2929; Fax: (802) 864-7626; www.bkconnection.com

Orders for college textbook/course adoption use. Please contact Berrett-Koehler: Tel: (800) 929-2929; Fax: (802) 864-7626.

Orders by U.S. trade bookstores and wholesalers. Please contact Ingram Publisher Services, Tel: (800) 509-4887; Fax: (800) 838-1149; E-mail: customer.service@ingrampublisherservices.com; or visit www.ingrampublisherservices.com/Ordering for details about electronic ordering.

Berrett-Koehler and the BK logo are registered trademarks of Berrett-Koehler Publishers, Inc.

Printed in China.

Berrett-Koehler books are printed on long-lasting acid-free paper. When it is available, we choose paper that has been manufactured by environmentally responsible processes. These may include using trees grown in sustainable forests, incorporating recycled paper, minimizing chlorine in bleaching, or recycling the energy produced at the paper mill.

Library of Congress Cataloging-in-Publication Data
McDargh, Eileen.
  Gifts from the mountain : simple truths for life's complexities / Eileen McDargh. — 1st ed.
    p. cm.
  ISBN 978-1-57675-469-6 (hardcover : alk. paper)
  1. Nature. 2. Life. 3. Mountaineering I. Title.
QH81.M1515 2007
508—dc22   2007014808

First Edition
12 11 10 09 08 07   10 9 8 7 6 5 4 3 2 1

To Contact Eileen: E-mail: eileen@eileenmcdargh.com, web: www.EileenMcDargh.com or call 949-496-8640
Book design by Whitney Campbell • Phone: 207-846-0768

Foreword

As a National Geographic photographer, I've worked for years to train my eyes and senses so I can capture moments of beauty and significance on film. What I do with a camera, Eileen has done with her words.

This is a book of rare wisdom and relevance. Having spent much of my life in wilderness, I know the quiet, deep teachings of nature. I also know it can take time and effort to find them. How marvelous that Eileen takes us on a trek with her, sharing the lessons she has found so that we can apply them in all parts of our life. Relax—you don't have to leave your chair.

Photographer John Muir insisted that we must "climb the mountains and get their glad tidings." Eileen hears all those "tidings" loud and clear and tells them in elegant language that can help us uncover ways to make our lives better, deeper, and richer.

Gifts from the Mountain captures the essence of what my camera lens finds—a banquet of wisdom for those who would listen and learn!

What a gift.

> Dewitt Jones, Award-winning National Geographic photographer,
> author, and acclaimed professional speaker

Come join my journey

and get ready for yours.

Eileen

Prologue

Gifts from the Mountain
Simple Truths for Life's Complexities

Years ago, my ideal vacation would have been found pool-side: comfort at my beck and call, hot showers, cold drinks, a suitcase filled with resort wear, and stacks of books on hand to read.

Hah! The fates had not warned me that I would fall in love with a man who would stick his nose in the calendar in January, point to a two-week time frame in mid-summer, confirm the phase of the moon (waxing) and announce his intent to apply for a wilderness permit. In my naiveté, "wilderness" meant back roads, drive-in restaurants, or getting lost and having to ask directions. But to Bill it was the vast 150 million year-old Sierra Nevada range running down the spine of California.

And so we went. Again and again.

In the course of our double-digit marriage, I've done my best to hang in there. Little would my clients and audiences guess this high-heeled speaker in corporate attire could emerge from Sierra Mountain passes, alpine meadows, ice fields, horrific storms, and below freezing temperatures with two weeks worth of grime, assorted cuts, bruises and bites, matted hair, swollen eyelids (altitude and sun always do it to me), and a strange mixture of unabashed relief and pride.

And then the inevitable happened. The children left home. This was the summer Bill and I would make our first ever twosome ascent into the Sierras.

No problem…except for the fact that with at least three people, the weight of equipment can be equally shared. No problem…except that I'm small and my backpack limit is about 35-40 pounds, but this time I'll need to carry more.

As we struggled over boulder-strewn fields, trudged up unmarked mountain passes at 12,000 plus feet, sidestepped across ice fields, watched 65 mph winds pick up a tent and soar it across granite towers, guzzled our last drop of water, praying we'd last until Coldwater Creek, I figured there HAD to be a reason behind this most difficult of trips. Perhaps this backpacking trek was in my life for a purpose.

So I began to pay attention, to see and hear with new eyes and ears. Surely this mountain had lessons to teach me, to force me to slow down and learn more by noticing more.

Who would ever have thought there'd be gifts in grime, grit, and grace-filled mornings? I found lessons for business, for relationships, for family, for life, and for my soul. It is my hope these lessons find a home in your world as well.

Life is complicated and complex. We yearn for simple answers and want them in sound bites, in small passages potent in message and meaning. This book seeks to answer that need. In many ways, it will remind you of what you already know but have forgotten in the tension of time constraints, work worries, and family

frustrations. Some passages will jar your memory while others might evoke a
new awareness and result in action.

You, too, have your own mountain. There's always a challenge that demands
your attention or a complication looking for simplification. Whether your complex world is the boardroom or bedroom, there are insights for the taking. May I
invite you to read while thinking of the places we all trek on a daily basis: those
places where we climb the corporate ladder, scale the next problem, surmount
the competition; those places where we forge streams filled with relationships
and pack bags crammed with "stuff"; those places where we think our journey
belongs only to ourselves and cast blind eye and deaf ear to the other people
along our trails; and lastly, those places which refresh and renew us for the next
climb, the next assault, the next mountain.

Open to any page. You don't have to read in sequential order. Ask yourself how
a simple truth can be extended as a tool in your life. If you so choose, pose the
statement to your work team, to your family, to your organization. Listen. Their
responses might turn a mountain into a molehill.

Come take a hike and discover your own footnotes for walking through life.
There is so much wisdom, hidden in plain view. Pause, look with new eyes,
and discover simple truths that can unravel and make sense of many of life's
complexities.

Climb the mountains and get their good tidings.

Nature's peace will flow into you

as sunshine flows into trees.

The winds will blow their own freshness into you

and the storms their energy

while cares will drop from you

like the leaves before Autumn.

—John Muir

Steady strides

beat hasty starts.

Backpacks have to settle.
You adjust here, tighten there, shift weight down,
shift weight up. It's a trial and error method as all
the while you maintain a steady, even pace.
No speed. Just walking, feeling, assessing.

Recall getting a new job, working for a new manager,
becoming a parent, or starting a relationship.
Too often mistakes are made at the outset because
we did not take time to walk steady, to feel, to assess,
to adjust here, to tighten there and loosen here.

Ignore the small pains, the momentary twinges
at your peril. They get bigger over time.

Honest adjustments are easiest in the beginning.
Pay attention. Easy does it.

Acclimate at a higher level
before you begin the next part
of the climb.

We're not only creatures of habit, but our physical bodies attempt to adjust to altitude and temperature. Even driving to a higher elevation can bring dull headaches and stomach discomfort. Add strenuous exercise to the mix and you can get an unpleasant case of altitude sickness. Go slow, drink water, stay at the new level and listen to your body. See how it feels. Sometimes bodies don't adjust and you're smart to head back down.

Have you ever aspired to go "higher" in life and then, after you worked so hard to achieve it, found that it did not sit well? Before you buy the bigger house, go for the advancement, seek the huge new client, mentally try it on. Better still, see if you can "sample the altitude". You can spend time in another department, maybe even shadow the president to see if you're a fit for that role. Before you buy the larger house, walk the neighborhood, talk to the neighbors. Try it on. Ask the huge client for a project assignment and learn what it will take from you AND from them.

If it feels right, go forward. If not, there's wisdom in turning around or staying where you are.

Switchbacks are necessary

to reach the top.

Mountain switchbacks—those S-shaped trails
that bring a backpacker slowly to the pass—can be wearisome.
Dust rises and walking far right to turn around and
trudge far left seems long and tedious.
Surely scrambling hand-over-hand is quicker.

Maybe yes. But more often it's dangerous and
can land you in a place where you cannot move. Shortcuts
do not often produce the result you expect.

There's a price to pay for not working the plan and planning
the work. We don't have to jump to "the top" now. Earn it:
effort repeated, over and over.

Pack out your garbage.

And while you're at it, don't forget the garbage
you might be tempted to leave when you pack out
of a job, a marriage, a relationship, a neighborhood.
Don't leave behind hurtful words,
discounted colleagues, spiteful after-the-fact stories,
trashed property or people.

Leave well. Someone will enter the spot you have left.
May there be no garbage left behind. Besides,
who knows? You might return someday.

Watch for "ducks"
and leave some behind.

Small pillars of rock, piled carefully by human hands,
are "ducks" and a backpacker's clue as to where
the trail turns. When a trail seems to offer too many
routes or disappears altogether, we look for these piles
ahead of us. Most of the time we learn our way
from the people who went before us.

If you blaze a new path, let others know
how you traversed the "mountain." The "ducks"
will get them started. Share your wisdom.

Sometimes, it's easier

without a pack.

We don't always need to carry the weight
of possessions with us. Exploring new territory,
the next ridgeline, a mountain stream, is easiest
when we are unencumbered.

Emotions can weigh as much as possessions.
Anger, jealousy, and fear can hold us back.
As we forge new relationships, life directions
or professional challenges, ditch this pack.

What are you carrying that you don't really need?

Alpine flowers bloom
where you least expect them.

Above the tree line, bitter Arctic winds scour
granite escarpments. The uppermost reaches of the
Sierra lie buried for months under ice and snow.
Yet for the few months of summer warmth, tiny blossoms
burst forth from a grayscape of unforgiving rock
to relish their moments in the sun.

The human heart blooms where you least expect it:
Winds of destruction, disease, war, poverty, divorce,
and death can blast humanscape and yet,
beneath it all, are moments of joy, love, kindness,
and great beauty. As Camus wrote,
"In the midst of winter, I finally learned that
there was in me an invincible summer."

You can't tell how far it is
until you begin.

Distance is deceiving.

What seemed so far is sometimes an easy jaunt.

On the other hand, the pass with ant-sized people
trudging across a high path looks easy until we discover
the treacherous curves of hidden boulders and switchbacks
buried beneath a slick, heart-sickening wall of snow.

After hours of fright, we emerge at the top.

The inner mountain valley lies green and welcoming.

You never know how far—or how hard—
until you begin. The commitment IS to begin.

Turn around.

Celebrate how far you've come.

Step after step. Past the manzanita bushes
and up through the aspen groves. Higher and higher.
The next thought is to find camp, and figure
what's for dinner.
Tired. So tired. And also proud.

We look at the map. How much distance?
How much elevation? And that difficult boulder field!
We made it—to tonight—to sleep.

How often do we fail to stop and celebrate
how far we've come? Turn around and celebrate.

P.S. If you've forgotten how far you've come,
ask your mother.

Pause and rest but don't stop.

Take the pack off. Enjoy the surroundings.
But mark your calendar for when you'll start back
up the trail. Get too comfortable and the weather
closes in. You could be stuck. Hanging out at
base camp is fun but it won't get you
over the summit.

Get your bearings
or you might end up someplace
you don't want to be.

There's nothing like heading down a trail
only to find, far later, that you've taken the wrong turn.
Once you're on a roll, it takes discipline to check
the compass and map. It's much easier (so it seems)
to forge ahead. Ask "Is this where I intended to go?"
Your gut speaks louder than your head.

Nothing will break your heart faster
than discovering you climbed
the wrong "mountain."

Solitude

lets you see more.

A day hike in spring, unfettered by the chatter of anyone
around me, brings a variable feast when I stop and sit.
Alone. Quiet. I climb through a field of pale blue larkspur,
past violet thistle heads, and yellow/orange poppies
to sink into thick, soft, foot-high grass.

Dozens of ladybugs climb stalks of waving green.
The earth plays the music of mourning doves supported by
crickets fiddling and mockingbirds whistling,
while the hum of tire music rises
from the road far below.

Meadow grasses bend before the morning breeze
making wave-like swells of pale green, white green,
spring green across the fields. And to think
I could have missed this banquet of beauty!

Our fast-paced, noise-choked world seems
to give us little space to be alone.
Take yourself away—and sit in solitude.
The table is ready for the feasting.

Every ounce counts.

Hike enough and you trim the weight
of what you carry. You learn that pita bread
weighs less than squaw bread; dried apples weigh less than
trail mix; ramen and dried vegetables weigh even less
than some freeze-dried entrees. You discover
you can share a tube of toothpaste. Ditto deodorant,
sunscreen, and bug repellent.

How often do we encumber our civilized life with things
we WANT instead of things we truly need?

Choose what you carry carefully.
I never saw a hearse with a U-haul behind.

Little things trip you up.

Boulders I can see;
it's the hidden root or the tiny stone on a
rocky trail I miss. Life is all in the details.
It's the careless gesture that invites or pushes away.
It's the forgotten thank-you note rather than
the big gift that is remembered.

Big things take care of themselves.
It's the pebble in the boot that causes the pain.

The flexible survive.
The yielding win the day.

Hike the Sierra and the force of nature throws itself
into your face at every turn. Granite slabs sprawl
like sleeping giants, their sides offering evidence of
the high mountain place from which they fell.
Towering trees thrust lightning-scarred arms
into the heavens.

How instructive then to find gentle alpine grass,
wee clover flowers and fragile columbine at elevations
hardest hit by severe storms and winter winds.
Surely there's a lesson here for all of us.

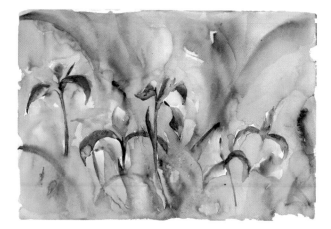

Walk too fast
and you'll miss the beauty.

Head down, intent upon
making it to the next marker, you miss
the spider's web cased in frost,
the ouzel bird walking on the river bottom,
the wild onions growing creekside,
the shooting star finger-painting the night sky,
the tiny tiger lily behind a rotted log,
the hummingbird on a high altitude bombing run.

In our hurry-up, instant-demand world, we miss
the dew on the spider web festooned across the walkway,
the children playing ball in their yard,
the mushrooms riding a sea of grass after days of rain,
the garden flower gracing a desk,
the burst of sun spraying the ocean.

One day, we'll lift our arms to heaven
and beg for just one more minute.
Stop and take it. NOW.

Sometimes it's better
not to know how hard the trail
or how far you have to go.

Optimism sets the pack on our back.

Adventure sets our foot on the path.

If we had been forewarned, our "logical" self

would have talked us out of the running.

We would never open the business, have the child,

write the book, or audition for the play.

We'd stay safe, comfortable, and comforted

in the knowledge that we "didn't bite off

more than we could chew."

Oh what delicious experiences we might miss!

Stop when you're tired.

Accidents happen when you push
beyond endurance. Mistakes arise when brains
are clouded by fatigue or pain. The law of diminished
return prevails: the quality of our efforts
becomes less and less.

Listen when your body speaks.
Put up the string hammock between the trees
and rest.

There's always tomorrow.
And if tomorrow doesn't come,
you'll have had a better today.

Mosquitoes
are only a nuisance.

Depending upon the amount of rain and
the elevations, we KNOW we'll have these whining,
buzzing, biting critters. So we're prepared:
heavy-duty repellent, mosquito netting for the head,
and a mosquito dance when it gets really annoying.
(The "dance" is a hopping variation-on-a-theme
created one summer when there had been
a lot of rain!)

Get used to them.
We'll always have the equivalent
of mosquitoes in our lives:
the always whining colleague,
the nit-picking relative,
the neighbor with the irritating habit.

Protect yourself and ignore the whine.
It's a nuisance but it's not going to stop you.

Feel the fear
and do it anyway.

Bathed in the umber glow of sunset, my body sinks
wearily into the sleeping bag. Exhausted, my mind replays
the day's journey marked by multiple scrambles
through boulder fields in a vain effort to find the trail.
Crossing the snowfield with its vertical slope
sliding ominously into a frozen lake had taken a toll.
Bill lost his footing and for a brief time,
I imagined him hurling into frigid waters,
held down by an 80-pound pack.

I inched back to help him, my legs quivering in cold
and the awkward angle of side stepping so as to
maintain balance against the snow-covered slope.
We crawled to safety after passing under an ice ledge
with a crack that threatened to widen any minute.

Suddenly, I sit up—wide awake.
I am terrified of falling, of dealing with icy surfaces.
And yet, I did it!

What could each of us do at home, in work,
if we stepped into the fear?

Observe nature's pattern.

Different trees grow
at different elevations.

And so do we.

Some of us belong with the giant redwoods
and the sequoias, breathing in the heady air,
towering above the landscape.
Others are like aspens, spreading roots and
creating a community of shimmering likeness.
Some are the prickly cactus variety,
singular in our place, holding moisture in,
yet blooming in the kindness of spring rains.

Nature always know best.
As my fellow writer Jim Cathcart says,
"Nurture your nature."

Look for ways
to make the trip enjoyable.

It doesn't have to be difficult all the time.
Plan a few days at base camp
to relax and fish.
Explore. Sing songs at night.
Bring a constellation
sky map for tracking the night sky.

Life is a trip.
Bring your version of fun into
your home, your office.
Try impromptu gatherings,
spur-of-the moment picnics,
candlelight for no reason,
a frivolous purchase that makes
your heart sing. Balance the effort with
joy and celebration.
Your fellow travelers will thank you.

Encourage those on the way up.

You saw it in the distance: the lower dip
in the mountain ridge that heralded Kearsage Pass
and your opening into the next basin. Once you've hit
the pass, you remember how you felt climbing up.
You see the pain and weariness in the hikers
trudging in your footsteps.

You remember what it was like as
a new employee, a struggling parent,
and just-promoted manager.
A word of encouragement can go a long way…
maybe all the way… to the top.

Downhill is more dangerous
than uphill.

What a relief, heading merrily down the trail.
My feet move faster on a down slope.
I gaze in the distance. I hum a tune. I crash,
my boots skidding on scree.
The tiny rocks-on-rocks act like ball bearings,
carrying my body along an uncharted path
bound for the oblivion of a steep ravine.
Thankfully, I stop myself by grasping
a sturdy shrub.

Cockiness takes over when it becomes easy.
Watch for the downhill.

If the sky falls,
there's another one behind it.

At 11,000 feet, Muriel Lakes is hit with
a two-hour hail and lightning storm the likes
of which I have never seen. Thunder bounces across
the granite rocks and lightning stitches
the early evening sky, connecting heaven and earth.

I am alone and terrified, huddling in a plastic tube tent,
wincing each time ice pellets hit my hand or head.
The world is a downpour of frozen rain and noise.

Finally, the ice and light show slides down the valley.
The night sky turns into a jumble of stars with
a slivered moon pierced by the sharpest mountain.

How good to remember: this too shall pass.

Watch for wild onions.

Until I joined my husband's backpacking treks,
he never realized that wild onions were there for the
taking. Added to noodle soup, the tang of spring-fed
tubers brings life to an otherwise ordinary dish.

We've all got "wild onions"
that can add zest to the journey:
wild ideas,
wild plans,
wild flowers,
wild moments of wild abandon.

You just have to know where they are
and how to use them.

If you keep your head inside a tent,
you'll miss the stars.

There's safety in your shelter.
But there's also utter darkness.

Stick your head out. Better still,
take your body with you and watch the stars twirl
across the galaxy. Create moonbeam dreams and
sing to the bat that silently, swiftly swoops in the gray night.
You will find another world of wonder
if you leave your tent.

You can be the bold human who knows
that embracing the night creates an even brighter dawn.
Take courage. You can always go back inside.

Don't keep looking for the pass.

Just go one step at a time.

The switchbacks lay beneath a few feet of snow.
A rope hoist lowered by two of our more intrepid
team members had us shinnying up the ice wall.
Far in the distance, across a snowfield,
I saw the small figures of trekkers making their
cautious way across the face of the cliff to the pass.
My heart sank. How could I ever make it?

One step at a time.
That's how each of us achieves our goals.
Concentrate on what is immediately in front of you—
not how far you have to go.

The careful steps NOW make the pass
come quicker—and safer.

Expect the unexpected

and deal with it.

It is how it is. Sharp wind. Freezing rain.
Blistering sun. Hard ground. Impassable creeks.
An inedible whole-wheat, dehydrated mess of garlic pasta.
All unpleasant. Unexpected.

But then sometimes the unexpected is
nothing short of a miracle: the moon orb that blazes
after a ferocious hour of hail; the blade of grass
encased in a jewel of ice; the discovery of mountain trout
in a remote lake. It is how it is.

It's worth the unpleasant unexpected to
appreciate the unexpected miracles.

Pain means the pack
must be adjusted.

Pain begins as a whisper that something is wrong.
Ignore the whisper and it becomes a shout.
We all carry weight in our lives. Alter it.
Shift the burden, adjust a strap, ask for help.
Sometimes it means leaving things behind
or trading packs.

Don't go on in pain.

No need to be a martyr.
Besides, canonization takes centuries.

Sometimes you have to
get your feet wet.

There it is. No doubt about it.
You can see the trail on the other side of the
rapidly moving creek. You walk up and down the
bank, searching for fallen logs straddling the water.
You look for stepping-stones jutting out of the stream.
Nothing. If you want to continue on the path
you've chosen, it means wading across
the cold stream fed by snow melt.

Life gives you choices.
You can stay on one side and keep your feet
warm and dry. Or you take the plunge
for what you want. What's worse:
to err for the things you did
or to err for the things you failed to do?

It always takes longer

than expected.

The perfect campsite is rarely around the next bend.
More often you scout out the territory and,
by process of elimination, determine the site.

An overnight success is never exactly "overnight."
Contractors always take longer than they estimate.
And when you're headed home,
it is never near enough.

The less you expect, the more you can handle.
Stay focused on the outcome,
not on the timetable.

Protecting the environment
is a nuisance.

Not having the environment
is a disaster.

Washing dishes far away from water sources,
packing out garbage, digging latrine holes, and using
a tiny stove instead of a fuel-burning bonfire
are all bothersome, time-consuming, and essential.
The wilderness environment would suffer.

We have everyday environments to protect:
washing language that soils the listener,
packing out old resentments, digging holes to bury anger,
deferring to collaboration instead of confrontation.
Not protecting this environment sets an organization,
a family, a community, into an inevitable downfall.

Big winds don't always
bring rain.

Skies darken. The wind shifts. Trees bend against the force and whitecaps speckle the lake. Ominous. Threatening. It's as if Mother Nature seeks to push us away. We wait to see what really happens.

Nothing.

There are experiences and people just like this – intimidating and threatening. Calmly watching and waiting lets us determine our response.

Remember the night rainbow.

Despite the steady sprinkles,
the moon plays hide and seek
with the rain clouds.
If I had vision for piercing the night,
I know the refraction of light
against the prisms
of earth-bound water
would cast a rainbow against the sky.

Just because I can't see it
doesn't mean it's not there.

That's faith.

You have to get your hands dirty.

Backpacking is not for the clean-of-palm
or the flawlessly manicured. Not, that is, if you're going
anywhere that requires more than an overnight hike.
Not if you want to discover fresh beauty and
sights reserved for a few.

You get your hands dirty caring for children,
mending a broken heart, cleaning your
mother's kitchen, taking your neighbor for chemo,
or holding a friend's hand while he or she
departs this life.

Be willing to get messy with life.
You'll discover rare beauty reserved for a few…
and the true gift of love.

You can do more than you think
you can, particularly when someone
believes in you. And especially
if you believe in yourself.

I can barely see the tip of Mt. Whitney, the highest mountain
in the lower 48 states. Although I have been assured that
an ascent after two weeks in the high country and
at higher elevations would make it an easier climb,
I have my doubts. My family doesn't;
they see more in me.

On THIS day, we're slowly walking single file on a narrow path
toward the summit. Despite a few days at 12,000 feet,
nausea slams into my stomach. I crouch behind a boulder,
violently ill. Other hikers are coming up the trail.
There's nothing to do but move forward.

I hear my family's encouragement echoed by a small voice
in my soul. An hour later, we're at the top, greeted by an
80-year-old woman who says her birthday wish
was to climb Mt. Whitney.

Her spirit overrode the logical objections of her age.
Her own inner voice encouraged her.

You can face your fear
without going over "the edge."

Bill is the kind of backpacker who looks at a map,
finds the John Muir Trail heading due north,
and then points in a different direction exclaiming,
"I can't believe someone hasn't gone this way!"

We've bushwhacked through fallen stands of thick trees,
crossed slick snow fields, and been turned around in
blinding rainstorms. I'm not the most adept with
a pack on my back and weak ankles taking sidesteps.
My heart pounds and I mutter words of self-encouragement
when crossing a whitewater river on a log. You probably
talk to yourself as you make that sales call, ask for a raise,
challenge the legal system, or stand up to your partner.
The important thing is to know your limitations.

There are times reason outweighs bravado.
Taking the long way around rather than shinnying up
an escarpment is just plain smart.

Hum the moon down!
Sing the sun up!

"Without a song, the day would never end."
How I remember singing these words as a teenager, captured
by the notion that music becomes a friend
to help us on our journey.

Singing is what we do around a campfire,
along a trail, or softly at night in the cuddly warmth
of a sleeping bag. It makes dishwashing easier,
morning brighter, hearts lighter.

The Australian Aborigines believe the voice should be used
first and foremost for song. As a people famed for
their walkabouts in the outback, perhaps singing has helped
them survive in a place of challenging geography,
extreme climate, and human misunderstanding.

As long as song is in our hearts,
we're on the right road.

Respect the territory
of the other animals.

"Bears don't go above 10,000 feet,"
proclaims my husband. And, with my fear of these hairy beasts,
I mutter, "So they can read an elevation marker?"

We've watched backpackers trek out from 10,500 feet
because bears took their supplies. We've heard tales of
a sow and cubs raiding camps in the backcountry.
And why not: this IS their land.

Human beings have their territory too.
When we intrude upon another's rightful domain,
an area of responsibility, a relationship –
even well intended –
the human animal gets upset.

Be mindful of territories.
Enter only when invited.

Let people know
where you're headed.

Backpacking in state or national wilderness areas
requires a permit. And when obtaining the permit,
you must also outline a general itinerary of your route.
We rarely follow it to the letter because
nature sometimes thwarts our best efforts.
But in case of emergencies, we've provided
at least some semblance of direction.

Too often, we hesitate to talk about what direction
we want for our lives. Maybe we're afraid others
will disagree or think us foolish. Or worse, we'll be held
accountable for what we have said is our goal!

If we don't share our direction, then how can
friends help us? Declare your intention
to people you trust.

Keep the naysayers in the dark.
Your friends will light the way.

Write on
keeps you right on.

Reach the end of a trip and the past few weeks
are a blur of sights, sounds and conversations.
Reach the end of a year and the
common sentiment is, "Where did it all go?"

Writing captures life in a few words
and can hold it precious. Before sleep creeps
into your brain, take a few minutes and
write a reflection of the day. Note what captured
your attention, whom you saw, what decisions
you made and what you are grateful for.
At the end of the year, you'll be surprised to realize
how full your life has been. You'll also sense
if you are headed in the direction you want to go.

Write on.

Wind rises most when
you're naked.

Dirt settles in wrinkles you didn't know you had.
Grime encircles the tops of socks.
Sand sticks to sunscreen and mosquito repellent.
You yearn for a hot shower.
But you'll gratefully settle for lukewarm water
from solar water bags hung from
the branch of a tree hidden behind a boulder.
The minute you get wet, count on it:
wind begins to blow.

Life often resembles that shower.
No one wants to be vulnerable but at times
we are—without the protective covering of job title,
status, sure knowledge, or predictable structures
and patterns. But even in the moments
of vulnerability, we can do what needs to be done
and ultimately "come clean" in the experience.

Don't forget the Band-Aids.

Sounds like silly advice and far too obvious.
Unfortunately, what we most often forget are the items
that are commonplace. Blisters are part of the trek;
simple to handle if you are prepared
and agony if you are not.

From the workplace to the home front,
daily living can create blisters. These can be small spots
caused by rubbing people the wrong way,
by speaking without thinking, by gesturing without
considering the meaning. Apply the Band-Aids
of apology, concern, clarification, and listening.
Forget the Band-Aids and a blister
becomes a festering wound.

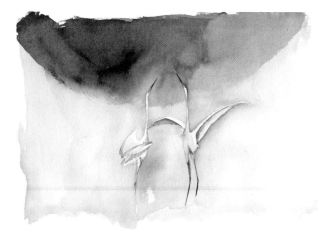

If someone is struggling,
share his load.

We all have different levels of strength
and different tolerances for weariness.
Today you are strong and can handle the load;
it takes but a minute to ease some of the burden
of a fellow hiker who is having trouble.

Someday, you'll need help.
It will all come back.

Travel with people
willing to share the work.

You are lugging a 20-pound bag of water
from the stream to the campfire where it will boil
and be purified. Although you've been on your feet
for hours, you also gathered the wood for the fire,
put out the sleeping bags, and cleaned the fish.
You return to the stream for more water.
Dishes need to be scrubbed away from
the water source and uneaten food
buried deep in the earth.

No problem except that the other hiker
just sits and watches you. She'll eat the food
and go to bed while you, like Cinderella,
finish the work. Not fair and not fun.

You have two choices. Talk it out immediately
and divide up the tasks. If that doesn't work,
just take care of yourself. Make sure YOU are not
the camp-sitter. To summarize Buckminster Fuller,
"On Spaceship Earth, there are no passengers.
We are all crew."

Look for help when you need it
– any kind of help.

I'm not very surefooted when crossing slippery logs
suspended across creeks or trying to boulder-hop and match
the strides of my tall husband. A plain, rubber-tipped
wooden cane steadies my efforts. What a helper!
I don't look as macho as the other people on the trail
who seem to leap rivers in a single bound, but who cares!

Are there times it's hard to admit you can't do it –
whatever "it" is – with the same nonchalance and
grace evidenced by others? You can get left behind
in life's journey if you don't look for resources
to match your ability. What "cane" could you use?

Cross the stream
if you come to it
– not before.

You can hear the roar of waterfalls before you see them.
The air gets cooler and the pungent smell of mud and pine
tickles your nose. Your mind creates a cataract of
gigantic proportions, a torrent of tumultuous whitewater
driven from some hollow home at the headwaters.
You become anxious about how you will cross such a force.

What's this? The trail moves away from the river.
You have to bushwhack through trees to even catch
a glimpse of it. And all that worry for nothing!

Laughter lifts your feet
and your heart.

When the trail is long and the campsite far away,
nothing beats a hearty laugh, a silly song,
and a quiet chuckle.

We've even resorted to reading the ingredients
of freeze-dried food as if we were
Jimmy Stewart,
John Wayne, or Scarlett O'Hara.
Pretty funny, Pilgrim!

You don't need as much food
as you think.

Hand us the dinner menu.
We'll order an appetizer, entrée and—well, if you insist,
dessert. The belt gets loosened a notch.
Eating is such a joy. Eating EVERYTHING is habit.

Isn't it amazing that oatmeal and dried apples
can carry you until a lunch. Lunch consists of more
dried fruit and maybe a half-piece of pita bread
and small piece of cheese. Dinner fits in a plastic
butter tub… a small butter tub. Swimming in
your yellow plastic cup are noodles, broth,
maybe freeze-dried meat and/or vegetables.
And it IS enough.

Here's the question:
where else do we overload our lives by habit?
What is enough?

Celebrate.
Celebrate.
Dance to the music.

At the end of our trek, we're fairly skipping down the trail,
loudly singing Zippedy Do Dah, or proclaiming
"I'm in a pizza state of mind" to a Billy Joel tune.
We've made it through.
Why not celebrate? Why not dance?

And why not? How often I lunge on to the next project,
the next to-do list, rather than celebrate what was just completed.
We wait until the year's end, until the last contract is signed,
or the kids graduate to holler "Alleluia" instead of
celebrating each step of the way.

I like to think that the natural world knows how to dance
and celebrate in the sheer joy of being alive, of having the gift
of another day. We can live our lives with that joy of celebration,
with the yahoo! moment of any small accomplishment.
We can sing and dance and celebrate the music and rhythms
of the world so that we tread lightly and lovingly
wherever we journey.

Celebrate today! Dance to your music.

There's no place like home.

In the literal sense, you rejoice to return
to your clean bed, your toilet, your clean clothes,
hot shower, long tub baths, razor, and refrigerator
stocked with cold drinks. You crave pizza, crisp salads,
potato chips, anything roasted in an oven,
and ice cream.

But that's not what I mean by "home."

Your home resides at the core of who you are.
It's that internal place of comfort that holds all your
joys and sorrows, your accomplishments and failures,
your deepest dreams and your deepest loves.
It accepts you and cherishes you as a vital participant
on the journey.

We spend a great deal of our life looking for that home.
The more we can look around us and see the signposts
and the trail markers, the more we can hear the messages
and the messengers, the more our journey
goes deeper and truer.

You'll know when you've arrived home.
Safe traveling.

Let the GIFTS go deeper.

There's more to this little book than meets the eye. You can find it a source of deeper conversations, innovations, insights, and candid dialogues.

I've created a series of **Conversation Fire Starters** that can be downloaded for free at http://www.eileenmcdargh.com/giftsfromthemountain.html and used to ignite you and the people around you.

If you are a manager, use *A Leader's Fire Starter Guide* to begin a meeting and delve deeper into issues and observations.

If you are a coach, use *A Coach's Fire Starter Guide*, to help a client discover a different way to look at the personal developments.

If you are a member of any discussion or support group, use *A Companion's Fire Starter Guide* to evoke unique responses from and revelations among your friends.

And since we are all on this journey together, I'd love to hear from you—not only how you have used this book but also about the metaphors that you now see and that carry meaning for you.
We can be teachers for each other. Write me at eileen@eileenmcdargh.com

About the Author

Since1980, Eileen has become noted as a powerful international keynoter who speaks the truth with clarity, wisdom, humor and compassion. Long-standing clients and repeat engagements attest to her commitment to make a difference in the minds, hearts, and spirits of organizations and individuals. For successive years, *Executive Excellence* magazine has ranked her as one of the top 50 thought leaders in leadership development.

She draws upon practical business know-how, life's experiences and years of consulting for major national and international organizations ranging from global pharmaceuticals to the US Armed Forces, from health care associations to religious institutions, from American Airlines to Xerox, from 3M to IBM, from drill foremen in the Arctic to juvenile offenders in prison

She authored *Work for a Living and Still Be Free to Live*, the first book on work/life balance – which continues to be published in revised editions. Subsequent books include *The Resilient Spirit* and *Talk Aint' Cheap: It's Priceless*.

Eileen is a certified speaking professional (CSP) and her selection into the Speaker Hall of Fame places her among the top 3% of the 4500-member National Speakers Association.

About Heron Dance

Heron Dance Press & Art Studio is a nonprofit 501(c)(3) organization founded in 1995. It is a work of love, an effort to produce something that is thought-provoking and beautiful. Through our website, quarterly journal, workshops, free weekly e-newsletter and watercolors, Heron Dance celebrates the seeker's journey and the beauty and mystery of the natural world.

We invite you to visit us at www.herondance.org to view the many beautiful watercolors by Rod MacIver and to browse the hundreds of pages of book excerpts, poetry, essays, and interviews of authors and artists. In our studio store, we offer Heron Dance notecards, limited-edition prints, and original paintings, as well as dozens of hard-to-find books, music, and films.

Artist Roderick MacIver

Artist Roderick MacIver founded Heron Dance in 1995 as a celebration of the gift of life. Heron Dance explores the seeker's journey and the human connection to the natural world. In his words:

"Wild places, places free from the influence of civilized humanity, inspire my life and art. Out there are cycles larger than the concerns of man. Out there exists a deep silence and deep peace, as well as, of course, a great struggle to hold on to the gift of life. With my art and life, I try to express reverence for the mystery and beauty of wild places."

"Watercolors are for me the perfect medium to express one's reverence for the great wildness. The delicacy and flow of the water medium inspires me to simplify, to minimize, to express the spirit and essence rather than the detail. I try and try and fail and over time, over months, over perhaps thousands of tries, I try with the hope that over time the spirit of that great flow might gradually emerge in my work."

Born in Canada, Rod currently splits his time between Heron Dance Press in Vermont and his home in New York's Adirondacks.

About Berrett-Koehler Publishers

Berrett-Koehler is an independent publisher dedicated to an ambitious mission: Creating a World that Works for All.

We believe that to truly create a better world, action is needed at all levels—individual, organizational, and societal. At the individual level, our publications help people align their lives with their values and with their aspirations for a better world. At the organizational level, our publications promote progressive leadership and management practices, socially responsible approaches to business, and humane and effective organizations. At the societal level, our publications advance social and economic justice, shared prosperity, sustainability, and new solutions to national and global issues.

A major theme of our publications is "Opening Up New Space." They challenge conventional thinking, introduce new ideas, and foster positive change. Their common quest is changing the underlying beliefs, mindsets, and structures that keep generating the same cycles of problems, no matter who our leaders are or what improvement programs we adopt.

We strive to practice what we preach—to operate our publishing company in line with the ideas in our books. At the core of our approach is *stewardship*, which we define as a deep sense of responsibility to administer the company for the benefit of all of our "stakeholder" groups: authors, customers, employees, investors, service providers, and the communities and environment around us.

We are grateful to the thousands of readers, authors, and other friends of the company who consider themselves to be part of the "BK Community." We hope that you, too, will join us in our mission.

A BK Life Book

This book is part of our BK Life series. BK Life books change people's lives. They help individuals improve their lives in ways that are beneficial for the families, organizations, communities, nations, and world in which they live and work. To find out more, visit www.bk-life.com.

Be Connected

Visit Our Website

Go to www.bkconnection.com to read exclusive previews and excerpts o
new books, find detailed information on all Berrett-Koehler titles and
authors, browse subject-area libraries of books, and get special discounts.

Subscribe to Our Free E-Newsletter

Be the first to hear about new publications, special discount offers,
exclusive articles, news about bestsellers, and more! Get on the list for
our free e-newsletter by going to www.bkconnection.com.

Get Quantity Discounts

Berrett-Koehler books are available at quantity discounts for orders of ten
or more copies. Please call us toll-free at (800) 929-2929 or email us at
bkp.orders@aidcvt.com.

Host a Reading Group

For tips on how to form and carry on a book reading group in your workplace or community, see our website at www.bkconnection.com.

Join the BK Community

Thousands of readers of our books have become part of the "BK
Community" by participating in events featuring our authors, reviewing
draft manuscripts of forthcoming books, spreading the word about their
favorite books, and supporting our publishing program in other ways.
If you would like to join the BK Community, please contact us at
bkcommunity@bkpub.com.